CLOSE WITH CONFIDENCE

TEXAS HOMEBUYERS 7 EASY STEPS TO THE BEST DEAL

by
CARL PIPOLY

Bloomington, IN  Milton Keynes, UK

AuthorHouse™
1663 Liberty Drive, Suite 200
Bloomington, IN 47403
www.authorhouse.com
Phone: 1-800-839-8640

AuthorHouse™ UK Ltd.
500 Avebury Boulevard
Central Milton Keynes, MK9 2BE
www.authorhouse.co.uk
Phone: 08001974150

First published by AuthorHouse 6/20/2006

ISBN: 1-4259-4133-8 (sc)

Printed in the United States of America
Bloomington, Indiana

This book is printed on acid-free paper.

To My Daughters Adyn and Gina,

My Sons Nathan and Jason,

My Wife Esther.

CLOSE WITH CONFIDENCE

CARL PIPOLY

SUCCESSFUL HOMEBUYING
IN
7 EASY STEPS

- **SAVE TENS OF THOUSANDS OF DOLLARS IN UNBARGAINED-FOR REPAIR COSTS**

- **CREATE INVALUABLE SECURITY AGAINST A BAD DEAL**

- **BUY A HOME YOU WILL ENJOY AND BE PROUD OF**

Contents

PROLOGUE

The Texas Real Estate Commission (TREC) has approved a number of standard forms that are used in the purchase and sale of residential properties in Texas. The One to Four Family Residential Contract (Resale) form or Earnest Money Contract form is used in virtually every residential real estate transaction that takes place in Texas. Real estate agents, brokers, buyers, and sellers all view the form as a necessity for accomplishing the purchase and sale of a home. Normally, none of the parties seeks out an attorney who specializes in the enforcement of these contracts, to advise them about the meaning of the language in the form. Because the form is approved by a state agency, most people have no reason to believe or suspect that the language in the form favors one party over another. A common feeling by all parties who use the form is that the language will protect them if there is a dispute. But that's not the case, as you will learn in this book.

The standard TREC Earnest Money Contract form is a multi-page (usually around fifteen pages), single-spaced document that contains numerous paragraphs under easy-to-understand headings. For example, going down the list of headings, one can find the following words: PARTIES, PROPERTY, SALES PRICE, EARNEST MONEY, PROPERTY CONDITION, CLOSING, and BROKERS. Real estate brokers and agents, of course, are familiar with these terms. After all, they work with these contracts on a daily basis. These terms by themselves are also easily understood by the general public in the market for a home. No hidden meaning exists in any of the terms. When the parties look over the form before signing, none of the headings — which are usually in bold type — raises any concern. The headings are familiar and they appear to cover a number of activities which a buyer and seller would expect to take place over the course of the transaction.

The easily understood headings give most buyers and sellers a level of comfort after reading the form. Unfortunately, those involved in a home purchase and sale normally do not wish to question their real estate agents or brokers over the precise meaning of the language that appears below the headings. This reluctance to raise questions may occur for a number of reasons: The parties do not wish to appear ignorant. They do not wish to appear to be giving the real estate agent or broker a difficult time. They want to trust everyone they are dealing with and don't wish to give anyone the idea that they mistrust them, for fear of upsetting them. All parties expect the form to afford them protections against an unscrupulous or untruthful individual.

Most real estate agents are very nice "people-type" persons. They are professionals who take time to meet with the clients at the home under consideration for purchase. While showing the client a number of homes before the client becomes interested in one, the real estate agent develops a relationship with the client. As the relationship with the real estate agent grows, the client begins to develop more and more trust in the agent. Usually, the agent is waiting at the home when the client arrives to see it. The agent tells the client the asking price and is the client's conduit to the seller for information. This relationship generates a certain amount of trust that grows to encompass the relationship: The more the client sees and talks with the real estate agent, the more the client wants to trust him or her. The agent is representing the client in what, for most people, is the single largest purchase they will ever make, so trust seems to be essential. This trust is not the kind of trust that is earned, say, by children from their parents. The trust in a real estate transaction arises from the act of working with an agent and knowing that the agent is a licensed professional. People tend to trust people who they themselves engage to represent them.

Significantly, when a buyer hires a real estate agent to assist with the purchase of a home, the agent isn't seen as a person who is looking out for the buyer's money. A buyer doesn't turn over money to an agent and then tell the agent to take the money and invest it in a house. For this reason, buyers normally don't do background or reference checks when hiring real estate agents, as they would if they were turning over $200,000 to a person to manage for their retirement. Then too, many real estate agencies advertise on television and radio, which tends to create trust in the consumer.

Once the house deal is closed at the title company, and the agent and broker are paid their commissions, however, the agent and the broker are out of the picture. There is nothing more for either of them to do in the transaction. While you may continually contact your money manager over time, especially if there is a problem with some investments, in the home-purchase scenario, once the deal is closed and the agent is paid, the contractual relationship with the agent is over. What this means is that buyers and sellers must take care to ensure that they fully understand their rights, duties, and obligations during the period of time from the initial hiring of the agent and broker through the closing of the purchase and sale. Although some real estate agents advertise they will help walk you through the paperwork, notably they are, by law, forbidden from giving their clients legal advice.

This book is intended to help ensure that you, as a buyer of a residential property, do not make a bad deal, and that you as a seller do not get sued because the buyer made a bad deal. There are *7 Easy Steps* that are vital for a buyer to follow when purchasing a home. If you as a buyer follow these steps, you will be happy with and enjoy the home you eventually decide to purchase and that you will not make a bad deal. Also, if you as the seller permit the buyer to follow these steps, you will not get sued by the buyer over a sale.

————————

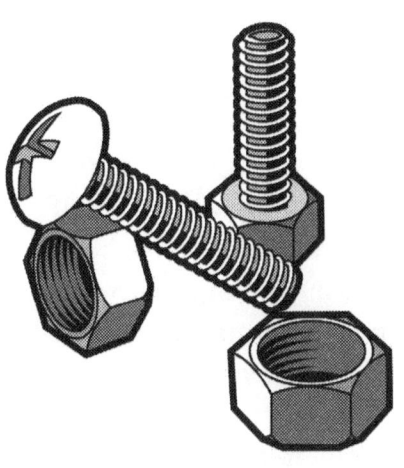

CHAPTER I

THE BASICS

When you begin thinking about purchasing a home, the first important item is, of course, the location. Where do you want to live? In the city? Near downtown? In the suburbs? Near good schools? Away from freeways? Near an airport, because you are constantly traveling? Whatever your criteria, think about it. Write it down. Discuss it with your spouse. Talk to your friends about it. Get comfortable in your own mind with the kind of area you want to live in. Be reasonable, however. Don't count on living in an area where the homes start at $3 million, if you only wish to spend $1 million. Once you have a good general idea of what part of the city it is that you wish to live in, you then must begin your search for a reputable home inspector.

Finding a good home inspector before you hire the agent is vital. It is essential that you take the time to do this as soon as you decide that you are going to enter the market for a home. You do not want to be looking for an inspector after you signed the earnest money contract and the seller has signed and accepted it. Once the earnest money contract is effective, the clock toward the closing date begins ticking. You want to call your inspector right away so that he can promptly get out to the home to perform an inspection. Chapter IV of this book will go over hiring an inspector in detail. Only after you have found an inspector that you will hire to inspect the home you will eventually place under contract, should you begin your search for a good real estate agent.

Searching for a good real estate agent is not particularly difficult.

Web sites, phone books, the real estate section of the Sunday newspaper, and signs in front of houses for sale are just some of the resources you can access as a start. Recommendations from friends and relatives are also a good source, as long as the persons recommended have the experience that you are looking for.

Real estate is booming all over the industrialized world. The boom is unprecedented. People in the U.S. are flocking to real estate courses offered to prepare them to pass the real estate exam so they can obtain a license to sell real estate. In many states, including Texas, applications for licenses to sell real estate have increased dramatically in 2005. People see all of the action and hear about all of the money being made in the residential market, and they do not want to be left behind. For buyers and sellers, however, this means a host of inexperienced real estate agents are flooding the market, ready to serve them. With all of the competition, it is a tough business. Only a small minority of these new licensees will achieve enough success to actually make a living. So it is important that you take the time to hire a reputable agent who knows the market in which you are about to purchase a home.

Do not hire a friend or a relative as your agent, unless the friend or relative has the experience you are looking for. My office has received a considerable number of calls from homebuyers involved in bad deals after engaging friends or relatives as their agent. This usually occurs when the agent is new and desperately needs to close a purchase and sale to meet his or her sales goals set by the broker they work for. The friendship sours. The buyer blames the agent for the bad deal. The buyer's agent blames the seller or the seller's agent. And it becomes a no-win situation for all concerned. Steer clear of this pitfall.

The most important bit of background information you want from the agent is how long he or she has been selling homes in the general area in which you are looking. You want an agent who is not just familiar with the market, but one who knows the market in the area in which you desire to purchase a home. You want one who has at least several years of experience in the particular market in which you are looking. I don't mean the broad general area. What I mean here is the *particular area* within the metropolitan area in which you want to make a purchase. If you want to purchase a home in a particular subdivision on the north side of your city, for example, you want an agent who has experience with homes sold in that particular subdivision. Simply representing buyers and sellers around the city is not good enough.

Once you have found several agents who qualify because of their experience in the particular area in which you are interested, then you must set up an appointment with each of them so that you can meet, go over your particular criteria, and hear what the market has to offer. Don't stop after you meet the first one. You must meet and visit with each one you have found with the right experience. Since they are all experienced, they will all be professional and knowledgeable. They will all be competent. They will all be sharp. But they will not all be the same. Based on their personalities and demonstrated dedication to assist you, one will stand out from the others as the one you want to hire. This is the one you should engage as your agent.

After you find your inspector and hire your agent, you can begin searching for your home. You know the kind of home you want in the location you want.

Do not accept anything less. Do not rush into an earnest money contract. Do not get pressured into signing an earnest money contract. You are spending your money. You are the one who is in control. You are the one who should make the decision of what home you want to put under contract. When you feel comfortable that you have found the home you want, you can then sign an earnest money contract containing an offer to purchase the home.

The amount of earnest money is always negotiable, but it is usually around $1,000 for, say, a $250,000 home. When a seller begins demanding more than a couple thousand dollars for a $250,000 residence, it could be a prelude to problems over the horizon. The more the earnest money demanded, the more skeptical the buyer should be. A large chunk of earnest money can strap a buyer into a very bad deal at the end of the day. You never want the loss of earnest money to pressure you into closing the deal. A good rule of thumb is never put up more earnest money than you can afford to lose if you must back out of the deal due to an unforeseen circumstance that does not permit you to cancel the contract.

Once the house is under contract, call your inspector right away, so that he can make arrangements to inspect the property. If a major problem surfaces, then you must figure out what you want to do. You can renegotiate a lower price or you can cancel the contract and get your earnest money back. If no major problems surface, you can begin moving toward closing the deal. The remainder of this book will show you seven easy steps to help ensure that you don't get ripped off, and that you close the deal with confidence.

———————

CHAPTER II:

STEP 1: BE PREPARED TO MAKE QUALITY DECISIONS YOURSELF. NEVER BUY A HOME SOLELY ON THE BASIS OF TRUST

Trust has nothing to do with the condition or quality of the home you are buying. Only objective reality matters. You may trust the brokers, the real estate agents, and the sellers to watch your children. You may trust them to the extent that you would not flinch at giving each one a personal loan. You may trust them to house-sit for you while you are away on an extended vacation. But chances are great that you would not trust any of these individuals to actually go out and select your dream home for you.

A home is a very personal purchase. It is also a very personal choice. Your home is your castle. You will live, eat, sleep, raise your children, entertain friends, relax, and enjoy life in the home you purchase. Think about this: Husbands and wives, in most cases, do not trust each other to be the only one who selects and purchases the home they will live in as their primary residence. This decision is made *jointly* by husband and wife, usually after lengthy discussions with each other and family and friends. When making such an all-important decision, you cannot afford to risk relying on trust or hope or faith to protect you against purchasing a defective property or a property that you will grow to hate because of problems you learn about after you close the deal.

Before you even take the first step in working with a real estate agent, be aware that the brokers, agents, and sellers involved in the transaction will provide you information about the property—which may or may not be accurate. Until you investigate the accuracy of this information, you will not and cannot know whether it is accurate. Therefore, do not rely on statements of agents or brokers or sellers about the quality and condition of the home. Find out for yourself.

Language used in TREC residential real estate contracts and in other documents used throughout Texas in residential real estate transactions unconditionally forbids you as a buyer from relying on representations made by the broker or agent because you had trusted them. These documents protect real estate agents and brokers against liability for misrepresentations about the quality or condition of the home being sold. For example, at the top of the Seller's Disclosure Notice is the following language:

THIS NOTICE IS A DISCLOSURE OF SELLER'S KNOWLEDGE OF THE CONDITION OF THE PROPERTY AS OF THE DATE SIGNED BY SELLER AND IS NOT A SUBSTITUTE FOR ANY INSPECTIONS OR WARRANTIES THE PURCHASER MAY WISH TO OBTAIN. IT IS NOT A WARRANTY OF ANY KIND BY SELLERS OR SELLER'S AGENTS.

On the second page of this document is a line for your signature. Immediately above the signature are words which state that you acknowledge receipt of the above notice. Once you sign the form, you represent that you have read and understood it. Should you purchase a defective home, you will not be able to say after the fact that that you didn't see the language above that tells you in all capital letters that the notice is not a substitute for your own inspection and is not a warranty of any kind by sellers or sellers' agents. This language is basically telling you to inspect the property yourself. It is language that substantially shields brokers and agents from liability for misrepresentations about the quality and condition of the home.

You can go to my Web site *www.pipolylaw. com* to find a copy of a blank Texas Real Estate Commission (TREC) approved Seller's Disclosure. If you look at page 1 at the top, you will find the above-mentioned language. In reviewing the other information in pages 1 and 2 of the form, you will see that the form covers virtually every part of the home. Any representations or misrepresentations that a broker or agent may make about the home will be covered by the Seller's Disclosure Notice. Putting it bluntly, you will not be able to blame the broker or agent for making a misrepresentation, even if they had made a misrepresentation. Why? Because the document you just signed states that all information provided in the notice was provided by the seller as of the date signed and is not a substitute for your own inspections. In addition, the document states that it is not a warranty of any kind by the seller or his agents.

The Texas Association of Realtors˚ uses a form called a Seller's Disclosure Notice, which exceeds the requirements in the one approved by TREC. Most likely, this is the form you will receive from the sellers. This form places even more emphasis on your duty as a buyer to inspect the property. It will contain language like the following:

> The brokers have relied on this notice as true and correct and have no reason to believe it to be false or inaccurate. YOU ARE ENCOURAGED TO

HAVE AN INSPECTOR OF YOUR CHOICE
INSPECT THE PROPERTY.

This language, or something similar, will appear on the last page of the form, immediately above your signature. Again, having signed the form right below that language, you will be unable to complain that the seller or his agent or broker had misled you about the history or condition of the property. These forms actually compel you to get your own inspector to inspect the property.

Next, at closing, you probably will be asked to sign what is called a Buyer's "Walk Thru" and Acceptance Form. This is another form used by agents or brokers who are members of the Texas Association of Realtors˚. Directly above the signature line at the bottom of the page on this form is the following statement:

The real estate brokers and the Seller have no knowledge of any defects in the Property other than what has been disclosed in the Seller's Disclosure Notice or other written information. The real estate brokers and Seller have no duty to inspect the Property for unknown defects. It is the Buyer's responsibility to have inspections completed.

You can see how the language at the end of the Buyer's "Walk Thru" and Acceptance Form ties into the language in the Seller's Disclosure Notice to form a tight barrier around brokers, agents, and sellers, to protect each of them from a damage claim by the buyer based on a misrepresentation. The protective language is contained in documents the buyer will sign in both instances. And it really hems in a buyer who discovers defects in the home after closing. Consider that the Seller's Disclosure Notice is provided to the potential buyer usually at the beginning of the transaction. This notice is usually provided to the buyer even before the Earnest Money Contract is signed. So, before a buyer even begins the process of purchasing the home, the buyer is on notice that he or she cannot rely on any statements made by the agent or broker about the quality or condition of the home, its systems, or appliances. From the start, the buyer is warned to conduct his or her own inspection. Then, at the very end of the transaction, the buyer again signs a document stating that it is the buyer's duty to inspect the property for defects. This is a spot you as a buyer do not want to get caught in after unknowingly purchasing a defective property.

In addition to being hemmed in by the Seller's Disclosure Notice and by the Buyer's "Walk Thru" and Acceptance Form, the buyer may be constrained from trusting the broker or agent by another form, the Residential Buyer/Tenant Representation Agreement. This form is also used by members of the Texas Association of Realtors˙. It sets out the relationship between you the buyer and your real estate broker or agent. The form is usually a two-page form and lists the buyer's and broker's obligations with respect to each other. It states what the broker's fees will be and identifies other areas of agreement such as limitation of liability, mediation, and attorney fees if a dispute arises. The form may also include a statement such as the following:

> Broker is not a property inspector, surveyor, engineer, environmental assessor, or compliance inspector. Client should seek experts to render such services for any property Client seeks to acquire.

And, as you may have guessed by now, this is another form that you will be asked to sign, and which you will sign if you want to have a real estate agent represent you — and you should have a real estate agent or broker represent you — in the purchase of your dream home.

In a residential real estate transaction, almost every time you sign something, some written language will be in the document telling you that you are responsible for searching for and finding defects in the home you're considering buying. Keep this in mind whenever you have concerns about the history, quality, or condition of the home.

Agents and brokers are not licensed home inspectors. These individuals are not trained to walk around the home and to look inside and out for the purpose of rendering opinions on the condition or quality of the home or any of its appliances or systems. Agents and brokers are required to use their best efforts to assist the buyer in locating a suitable property for purchase in an area where the buyer desires to make the purchase, and to assist the buyer in negotiating the purchase and sale. Basically, that is all a broker or agent is required to do.

In a sense, other than helping you negotiate the purchase price, the agent is like a search function on a computer. You type in certain words and then tell the computer to find the subject matter you want. For example, you're looking for a certain kind of antique chair. You go to the Google search engine, type in some words describing the chair, hit the search button, and up pops a number of Web sites that contain the type of chair you're searching for. The search engine is not responsible for the condition or the quality of any item presented. It is not responsible for providing you legal advice. It merely shows the person accessing the site where the item is located and how much it would cost to purchase.

Quality decisions must be made by you, based on what investment contracts refer to as "due diligence," or your own research as a buyer. You are the one who must determine whether the home is free of defects. If you are concerned about how the condition of any system in the home under consideration for purchase, you must satisfy yourself that the condition is acceptable to you. You cannot rely on the real estate agent to do this for you. The real estate agent, for purposes of this example, is not much different from the search engine on the computer when it comes to locating a property for purchase. You give the agent information, such as size of home, location, pool, ranch or split-level, age, proximity to schools, churches, athletic complexes, and so forth. The agent then takes this information and begins the search to find the type of home you're looking for in the area you want, at the price you wish to pay. Another thing to be aware of is that real estate agents are not lawyers. They are forbidden by law from giving you legal advice.

Once the agent finds one or more homes for you to view, based on the criteria you presented, the agent then begins the process of showing them to you. This is where you have to be careful not to rely on any statements that the agent makes about the condition and quality of the home, any of its appliances or amenities, or its structural or other components. This is because in most of the documents that you sign in connection with the transaction, you will affirm that you know, understand, and realize that your broker or agent has no independent personal knowledge about the home. The documents you sign reveal to anyone who reviews them that you understand that all of the broker's or agent's knowledge about the property was learned from the Seller's Disclosure Notice or from the sellers themselves. Your signature on the disclosure notice, on the Buyer's "Walk Thru" and Acceptance Form, and on the representation agreement verifies that you have not relied on any statements made by the agent or the broker about the condition or quality of the home.

At every turn, the documents you as a buyer sign in a residential real estate transaction place the responsibility for determining the condition and quality of the home squarely on you, the buyer. The written language in these documents will attach that responsibility to you completely. Once you sign these documents and close the deal, you will have effectively relieved the seller, agent, or broker from any liability for statements made to you about the quality or condition of the home.

By signing these documents, you have relieved the agent, broker, and seller from any liability arising from problems with the condition of the home or anything in it that you discover after closing. If you have purchased a home with foundation problems, structural problems, roof leaks, bad wiring, plumbing problems, or other impediments, you probably relied on trust to shield you from those problems. If this happens to you after reading this book, you will have only yourself to blame.

Follow *Step 1*. Know you are responsible for making quality assessments about the history and condition of home under consideration. Don't gamble that trust and hope will fulfill this responsibility. Begin your quest toward closing the deal for your dream home with the confidence of a pro.

CHAPTER III:

Step 2: The Home Is Being Sold "As Is." So Act Like You Buy It "As Is."

Even though the TREC form Earnest Money Contract does not clearly and specifically state that the home is being sold "AS IS," that is exactly how the home is being sold. This is because the courts in Texas as well as a number of other states have decided to interpret these state-agency-approved form contracts as "AS IS" contracts.

We all know what "AS IS" means. We learn this early in life when we go shopping with our parents and see "AS IS" signs. The meaning is the same across America, no matter what state you're in or what product you're purchasing. If we purchase any product "AS IS," we take the product just as we see it. There are no warranties or guarantees. There are no assurances that the product will even work. What we see is what we get, nothing more and nothing less. When we purchase something "AS IS," we take the risk that the product may not work properly. Usually, items sold "AS IS" will cost less than the same item that is sold with some kind of warranty or guarantee. When something is sold "AS IS," we have a general expectation that the item is of lesser quality and in poorer condition than one that is sold otherwise. The words "AS IS" place everyone who sees them on notice that the thing being sold should be carefully examined before purchase.

Although the courts in Texas and other states interpret the agency-approved form Earnest Money Contracts to be "AS IS" contracts, nowhere in those contracts will we find the words "AS IS." Instead, we will see that the contract provision interpreted to mean "AS IS" uses the words, "in its present condition." You may access a sample form Earnest Money Contract at my Web site *www.pipolylaw.com*. After you read that language, if you're like most of us, you will be surprised that this language means the same thing as "AS IS." While we are conditioned from our formative years to know and understand what "AS IS" means, most of us — even most real estate agents I have talked to regarding the Earnest Money Contract — have no idea that the courts have ruled that "in its present condition" means the same thing as "AS IS." This is understandable, since brokers and agents cannot give legal advice. So not only do the documents you sign in a residential real estate transaction forbid you from relying on statements made by the agents, brokers, and sellers, but the Earnest Money Contract you will sign shows that you are buying the property "AS IS."

The only time ordinary everyday homebuyers will learn of this hidden meaning is when they discover — after the deal is closed, usually within the first ninety days of owning the property — that what was actually purchased was not what was intended. Usually a problem is discovered and it will take considerable expense to fix it. It may be an air-conditioning unit that must be replaced; it may be a rewiring job; it may be a plumbing leak, a damaged roof, a defective foundation, rotting beams, poor drainage, or any number of other problems.

Virtually all purchasers who have sought assistance from my firm upon discovering they unwittingly had purchased a defective home insisted they had not purchased the home "AS IS," and that nowhere did any documents they had signed place them on notice that they were purchasing the home "AS IS." The common refrain is: "I never knew I had purchased the home 'AS IS.' Had I known the home was being sold 'AS IS,' I never would have paid that price for the home, or I never even would have closed the deal."

Because Texas courts have interpreted the standard form TREC Earnest Money Contract, used in virtually every residential real estate transaction that takes place in which the buyer is represented by a real estate agent or broker, as an "AS IS" contract, we as buyers must obtain as much information about the history, quality, and condition of the property we're about to purchase as we possibly can. The "AS IS" contract in and of itself requires that we gather this information. The other documents that we will sign, such as the Seller's Disclosure Notice, the Representation Agreement, and the Buyer's "Walk Thru" And Acceptance form, demand that we obtain this information.

Due to the responsibilities the contracts place on us for learning about the quality and condition of the property, we must have an opportunity to discuss the history, quality, and condition of the property with the sellers. Often, the only opportunity to get the information you need to make the right decision at the right price is directly from the sellers, in a face-to-face conversation. Normally, this should be a relaxed, sit-down conversation at which time we as buyers ask the sellers questions about the property that will assist us in deciding whether or not to purchase it, or whether or not to even place it under an Earnest Money Contract. This conversation is extremely important. It gives us an opportunity to meet and see the sellers face-to-face. Most sellers are decent, honest people who will be happy to share information about the property and will welcome such a visit, whether they presently live in the home and are moving elsewhere or they are investors who buy homes and fix them up for resale.

In these relaxed and informal meetings, we can learn a lot about the property we are thinking about purchasing that will not surface in the Seller's Disclosure Notice or in the Property Inspection Report that we will obtain if we decide to sign an Earnest Money Contract. For example, a simple question like, "Have you ever had any fuses blow out?" may reveal a wealth of information about the electrical system. A simple and direct "no" would give you an indication that nothing is wrong. A hesitation and then an answer that says "Yes, there was a time awhile back when we had a fuse blow during Christmas when we had too many lights hooked up to the system," will be cause for having particular attention paid to the electrical system during a more thorough inspection down the road. During this meeting, ask about all of the things that really concern you about the property. This is a vital part of your research, or "due diligence," as it is referred to in investment contracts.

Do not let your real estate agent or broker tell you that you cannot ask questions of the sellers. Information is essential for you to make an informed decision. Without information, you are vulnerable, especially when you consider that the Earnest Money Contract that you are about to sign, or which you have already signed, is an "AS IS" contract. The substantial amount of money you are about to invest in your dream home will be placed at high risk without the information. Buying a home without knowing essential information about the home is like buying a car "AS IS" — without looking under the hood to see if it has an engine, without starting it up to see if it runs, and without driving it. You would not think about doing that with an investment of $10,000 or $20,000. Why on earth would you consider doing that with an investment of $100,000 or more? Recent studies show that the price of the average home being sold in the U.S. is now $200,000.

If your real estate agent advises you that you should not ask the sellers questions or tells you that they will not see you, then you must get a new real estate agent or begin looking for another house, or both. When a real estate agent, broker, or seller does anything to stop or hinder you from gaining as much information about the history, condition, or qualities of the property as you feel is necessary to protect your investment, it is a warning that you should discharge the agent immediately. The agent who hinders you from getting information is looking to quickly close the sale for the agent's or broker's own benefit, not yours. The faster the sale closes, the quicker the agent and broker get their commissions. Your interest at this juncture is to get information about the property under consideration. Your agent is required to assist you in getting that information. You must take precautions to quickly terminate the representation contract you had entered into with an agent who is not representing your interests.

Fortunately, the majority of agents and brokers are honorable professionals with your interests in mind. These agents and brokers will do everything they can to assist you in obtaining all of the information you want to get about the home before closing the deal. They will not discourage you from diligently learning about the history of the property so you can make a decision to purchase that you will be happy with.

Therefore, professional agents and brokers will support you in getting as much information about the home for sale as you possibly can, so you can make an informed decision. A good agent wants your business the next time you purchase a home and wants you to refer business to him or her. Good agents will serve you and make sure your purchase is sound and made at a fair price. The majority of real estate agents and brokers are professionals who love doing their job, and it is not hard to find them. If your agent assists and encourages you to get information about the home, you have a good agent who is not out to trick you in the purchase of your home. Whether it is the first home you're buying or the tenth, you must get the information you need to make an informed decision before you close the deal.

Always remember that you are buying the home "AS IS," and all of the documents you will sign to close the deal make it your responsibility to search for and discover defects that you do not want to be saddled with fixing after closing. Applying the principles in *Step 2* to the search for the home you want will ensure the fulfillment of your duties and responsibilities as a buyer so that you can close your home purchase with confidence.

———————

CHAPTER IV:

Step 3: You Have A Right To Inspect—negotiate Sufficient Time To Do It

The TREC Earnest Money Contract contains a provision which permits you, the potential buyer, to inspect the home. Under this provision, the seller must give the buyer unlimited access to every portion of the residence and property for a reasonable amount of time to inspect the home. The potential purchaser can spend time in the home on a cold day by turning off the furnace and then determining how long it will take the home to heat back up to a certain temperature. The same test can be performed in the summer with the air conditioning to determine how long it will take the home to cool. When the home contains furniture, the buyer has the right to move furniture, or to remove paintings to check for defects in the walls. The sellers must make every inch of the home available for inspection, including cabinets, attics, basements, garages, fenced back yards with dogs, and utility rooms. All areas of the home and property must be made available for inspection. Statements such as "My aged mother is ill and cannot be bothered, so please do not go in the bedroom," or "Do not go in the basement because I have a dog that bites" are red flags. If you're confronted with such statements, you must then arrange a time when you can see the room containing the aged mother or the basement with the vicious dog, so you can thoroughly inspect those areas. If the seller refuses access, you *must* terminate the Earnest Money Contract. Refusing access for the purpose of inspection is not negotiable. Since all documents you will sign place the burden of inspection on you, the buyer, you must have access to the entire home.

There may be a blank in the Earnest Money Contract where you can insert a time period in which you must conduct your inspection. This is an extremely important provision. Many times, the agent will place ten days in this provision and the client will agree. But once you sign the Earnest Money Contract, this means you have only ten days to inspect the property. You will have to hire an inspector to inspect the home and report back to you, and then you will have to decide whether you still want to go forward with the purchase.

Do not get pressured into a short inspection time limit. Once you sign the agreement, it will be difficult to change it. Not impossible, but difficult. You read it, your agent read it, and you signed it. You will probably be stuck with the ten days. This means you have ten days to locate, hire, and arrange for a time when an inspector can come to inspect the home. Inspectors usually require three to five days or more for notice for an inspection. Once they inspect the home, they will need one to three days to provide you a written report. Often, the report is provided on the ninth or tenth day. I have even seen a number of cases where the inspection report was delivered to the buyer by the real estate agent after the inspection period had expired. Don't let this happen to you. It's your responsibility to make certain you have sufficient time to inspect the property.

You, as a home buyer, need time to read the inspection report — all of it — including the fine print. Then once you've read it and understand it, you must set up a meeting with the inspector to ask him or her to explain anything you don't understand in the report. Questions like "How serious is the problem?" or "Why did you recommend that we hire an engineer to check the problem?" or "You state here that the electrical system is in need of repair, specifically what is it that needs repair?" are the kinds of questions you must explore with the inspector.

You cannot afford to rush around on the day before closing, trying to locate and talk to your inspector. For example, the inspector may have recommended that an engineer be hired to inspect the foundation. You must discuss this recommendation immediately, before the inspection period expires. If you have to hire an engineer, then the time period for you to cancel the contract must be renegotiated, or you must terminate the contract, so you don't lose your earnest money. Once you have all of the information from the inspector, you must digest it and then make a determination how the information affects your purchase. You need at least several days to do this. In order to avoid being rushed into a short inspection time frame, I recommend that you insert in this inspection provision that you have a minimum of ten days *after* the inspector completes his inspection to review his report, during which you can terminate the Earnest Money Contract. This will give you time to read, review, and consult with the inspector about his report, and conduct any follow-up inspection you may need, such as hiring an engineer to inspect the foundation, and to renegotiate the expiration of the inspection period or your unrestricted right to terminate the contract.

If your Earnest Money Contract does not contain a time period for inspection, then it most likely will contain a provision which permits you to pay an option fee for the unrestricted right to terminate the contract within a certain time period. The cost of this option is negotiable, but usually it is around $100. If your contract does not contain a time limit for the inspection, then you must purchase this option in order to allow you the unrestricted right to terminate the contract. You must have this right so that you are not locked into a bad deal if you find after the inspection that you do not wish to purchase the home. By purchasing this option, you will protect your earnest money, should you decide to cancel the contract. If you purchase this option, then make certain you have time to go over the inspection report. Just like you would have done with the inspection time limit, you should make certain that the option gives you the unrestricted right to cancel the contract at any time within ten days *after* you receive the inspection report from your own inspector.

You have a right to ask for the utility bills. If you're concerned about the cost of utilities, ask for the bills in summer and winter. If the seller doesn't keep copies of the utility bills, then ask the seller for permission to obtain the bills from the utility company. I have a blank copy of a form on my Web site *www.pipolylaw.com* that you may download for this purpose. Once you submit the request to the utility company, it will take approximately two to three days for you to receive the information.

You can learn a lot from monthly utility bills. An excessively high water bill may indicate a plumbing leak in an incoming or pressurized water line. Higher-than-normal heating and air-conditioning bills may indicate a poorly insulated home or problems with the heating and air-conditioning unit.

If the home has had previous foundation or other repairs, request all documents associated with the repairs. You will want all warranty information, if any. You will want copies of the repair contract and, in the case of foundation repairs, the elevations and measurements taken of the foundation before it was repaired. You will want any photographs taken of the problem areas or cosmetic damages that needed to be repaired as a result of the problem. You will also want names and telephone numbers of the companies, engineers, electricians, plumbers, roofers, or other professionals involved in the repair process.

This is the same with any repair that the sellers have brought to your attention or which you find out on your own. You want all the information you can get your hands on about the repair, regardless of how the repair was made or what type of repair it was. Information about repairs performed on the home is critical to your understanding of the condition and history of the home. No one is required to give you this information. You must obtain it on your own. You must ask for it. You have a duty to ask for it.

When you are performing your duty and responsibility to get information about the home, you will want to know certain things about the history of the home or the condition of appliances or systems in the home. While I cannot list everything you will want to know here, I can assure you that you will have questions. These questions must be answered. If you do not ask, you will not get an answer, and more importantly, you will not have fulfilled your duty and responsibility to get the information necessary for you to make an informed decision.

Inspect the home. Ask questions. Get the answers. Make certain you have sufficient time to digest the information before getting locked into closing the deal. Follow *Step 3* and you will have performed your duties and responsibilities as you are required to. And, better yet, you can go to closing with the confidence that you have provided yourself the valuable protection necessary to shield you from a bad deal.

———————

CHAPTER V

STEP 4: HIRE YOUR OWN INSPECTOR

As I mentioned in Chapter I, you'll most likely sign the Texas Association of Realtors' Buyer's "Walk Thru" and Acceptance Form, either at the closing or right before the closing. This form will contain language to the effect that the property was inspected by an inspector of the buyer's choice, and that the buyer has reviewed the inspection reports. The first important thing you must be aware of regarding this language is that when you as a buyer sign the form, you are declaring that you—not the agent, not the broker, and not the seller—are the one who actually selected the inspector. Therefore, you must make the selection — not the agent, not the broker, and not the seller.

In many transactions my firm has handled for clients who complained about being misled about the condition or quality of a property, we have learned the inspector who inspected the property was recommended by the broker or agent. And unfortunately the clients did not discover the defects until after they had closed the deal and moved into the home. In this scenario, the agent will give the prospective purchaser — you — a list of inspectors. The list may contain the names of as few as one, and as many as ten or more inspectors. Indeed, my firm has run across a number of instances where the agent recommended a single inspector. Recommending a single inspector to a client who is the potential purchaser of a home is an absolute "no-no" for an agent or broker. Obviously, there is no choice when a single inspector is recommended by the potential buyer's agent. There isn't much of a choice either when just two or three inspectors are recommended by the agent. The plain fact is that when real estate agents provide their clients with lists of inspectors, they will only put the names of the inspectors *they* are comfortable with on the list. You're the one buying the house. You're the one who is going to be living in the house. It's your money that's being spent. You must be the one who is comfortable with the inspector.

Like the members of any other profession in a city or town, members of the real estate inspection profession gain reputations which the real estate agents are aware of. Some inspectors are noted for the cavalier way in which they inspect properties. These inspectors will almost never find anything major wrong with the home, such that the client would terminate the contract or refuse to close until the contract was renegotiated. If a major problem surfaces after the inspection, these inspectors will rely on the small print in their inspection contracts to protect them against any claim that they did not properly do their job. A famous judge by the name of Learned Hand once said, "What the large print giveth, the small print taketh away." This becomes glaringly true when a buyer attempts to hold a real estate inspector liable for negligently conducting an inspection of a residential property in Texas.

In reviewing the real estate inspector's contracts and the sample inspection reports, we see that the language in the inspection report is quite similar to the language in the Seller's Disclosure Notice. The TREC-approved inspection reports will contain the following language:

> The inspection is of conditions which are present and visible at the time of the inspection.

The Seller's Disclosure Notice approved by the TREC states as follows:

> THIS NOTICE IS A DISCLOSURE OF SELLER'S KNOWLEDGE OF THE CONDITION OF THE PROPERTY AS OF THE DATE SIGNED BY SELLER ....

Just as the disclosure notice is limited to the date the seller signs the notice, the inspection report is limited to the date and time of the inspection. Each document contains language which limits the information set out in each document to a small point in time. The inspection report is limited to an hour or so — however long the inspector was at the home — and the disclosure notice is limited to a single day. We as buyers must understand these limitations because we certainly don't want to be in a position down the road to have to recreate these points in time in order to make a misrepresentation claim against either the inspector or the seller. While such recreations are certainly doable, they are costly, time-consuming, and cumbersome. Then, once the recreation is complete and we have all of the evidence necessary to make and win a valid misrepresentation claim, we may discover that neither the inspector nor the seller has the financial wherewithal to pay a judgment. The TREC, for example, does not require real estate inspectors to carry malpractice or errors-and-omissions insurance. A lot of inspectors also include in their contracts a provision that limits their liability to the amount you pay for the inspection, which is usually between $150 and $300.

I'm not criticizing inspectors for having these kinds of contracts. Such contracts are perfectly acceptable in a residential real estate transaction, and in fact comply with the laws of the State of Texas. There's nothing sinister about an inspector limiting his liability in a contract. Nor is there anything sinister about TREC approving language in inspection reports which limits the scope of the inspection to the condition of the property on a single day. These limitations in inspection contracts are well and good. It's vital that we as buyers know these limitations and understand them when we hire an inspector to inspect the property we are about to purchase. Knowing and understanding these limitations will ensure that we utilize the inspection report for the purpose for which it was intended, and nothing more.

The reason you must not rely on your agent to recommend an inspector is that you state when you sign the closing documents that you hired the inspector or that the inspector was of your choice. If that is what is stated in the documents you signed, then you need to be very certain that you are the one who hired the inspector to conduct the inspection. This means that you must be the one who looks for, interviews, and hires the inspector. Do not rely solely on your real estate agent's recommendation. If, after closing, you discover a defect in the home that the inspector should have discovered but didn't, you will not be able to complain that you followed your agent's recommendation and relied on the agent's recommendation that the inspector was a good inspector and therefore it is your agent's fault, not yours. I assure you, your agent will answer that you did not have to follow his or her recommendation. Your agent will say that you were free to hire any inspector you wanted. Your agent will also point to the document you signed at closing, stating that you hired the inspector. Your agent will also point to the closing statement and show that it was you who paid the inspector's fee.

If you hire an inspector recommended by your real estate agent, make certain that you have checked the inspector's credentials, reputation, and background yourself. Do not rely blindly on the recommendation. You are about to make a large purchase worth tens of thousands, hundreds of thousands, and maybe even more than a million dollars. Take the time to hire a reputable inspector with a proven track record. Do not roll the dice. Hire an inspector you are comfortable with, one you can talk to, one who is experienced, and one you feel confident will get the job done properly. Real estate agents aren't permitted to recommend a single inspector. The choice is always up to you.

Hiring an inspector is an important part of any real estate transaction. It must be a personal choice. *You* must search for, interview, and hire the inspector — not your real estate agent. Don't rely on your agent for recommendations of real estate inspectors. In fact, do not even ask your agent for a recommendation. Take the few hours you will need to engage an inspector and go through the hiring and interview process yourself. Call at least three different inspectors and discuss their procedures with them. Find out what you can expect from them. You must be able to sit down with them and go over their report after you had an opportunity to review it. You will be making a very big purchase financially, so the minutes you spend going over the inspection report with the inspector will pay huge dividends down the road. Take the time.

Remember that the inspector is being paid from $100 to $300 for his services. For this kind of money, an individual cannot be expected to provide a client an inspection that would bring every problem to a client's attention. Inspection reports are worth what a potential homebuyer pays for them. However, most homebuyers could perform the same inspection themselves if they took the time. A full inspection, like one done by a professional home inspector, usually takes from one to three hours, depending on the size of the home. Turning lights on and off, turning water on and off, checking all of the appliances in the home, checking each faucet for leaks. Turning the hose faucets outside of the home on and off, and again checking for leaks. Checking to see if there are cracks in the drywall in any of the rooms. Checking under the sinks in the bathrooms, the kitchen, and the utility room for damp or moldy smells. Checking the water heater to see if it's old and rusty. Checking to see if there's an odor of gas around any of the gas appliances. Looking at all of the windows to see if they open, close, and lock properly. If there are storm windows, making certain all of the storm windows fit and that all of the windows that require screens have them. You are always permitted to attend the inspection as it takes place and I highly recommend that you do so.

The driveways and walkways around the home should also be inspected visually. Cracking in these may indicate the presence of expansive clay soils around the home. While the presence of such soils does not necessarily mean the home will have foundation problems, it may mean that if there is a below-slab plumbing leak, the home will suffer foundation problems. Below-slab plumbing leaks are a major source of foundation problems in homes built on expansive clay soils. Similarly, the buyer should check the floor of the garage for cracks. All garages will probably contain hairline cracks. These are not the kind of cracks which should cause concern. If the crack or cracks are larger than hairline and extend in the slab under the dwelling, then such cracks are an indication that there may be a problem with foundation movement.

Sellers, real estate agents, and others may say there's nothing to worry about. In fact, the inspector probably will say the house is safe for occupancy. Do not under any circumstances equate the fact that the house is safe for occupancy with the understanding that the house is free from foundation or other structural problems. The vast majority of homes that suffer from foundation problems are safe for occupancy. The problem with a home with foundation problems is that it has a negative stigma attached to it, which decreases the value. The foundation problem also causes cracking throughout the home, resulting in an unsightly appearance.

It's difficult, if not impossible, to sell a home with foundation problems for the same price per square foot as an identical home without foundation problems. People don't want to live in homes with foundation problems. The cracks in the walls, ceilings, and outer bricks are unsightly. They make a home look uncared for or unkempt. When cracks appear in a newly purchased home, they cause much heartache for the buyers. They see the major investment made for purposes of enjoying a gain or appreciation going down the drain. This usually leads to arguments between husband and wife about who wanted the home in the first place. From there, the home becomes the center of a contentious universe, which begins spinning in a downward spiral. Don't let this happen to you. Foundation problems are problems you should get information about and be concerned about if you have any idea at all that the home suffers from such problems.

If you are concerned about lead-based paints, mold, asbestos, radon gas, or other contaminants or environmental problems the home may have, then you must investigate to see if such problems do, in fact, exist. Just because no one mentioned such problems to you does not mean that such problems do not exist. The sellers, agents, and brokers involved in the sale of the home are not required to make determinations that the home is free of such contaminants before the home is sold. As you recall from Chapter II, the home is being sold "AS IS." So if you are concerned about these kinds of things, then you must spend the money to have a professional inspect for them. The cost of the inspection will be far less, probably thousands or tens of thousands of dollars less, than the cost of remediation and repair.

Remember the statement in the Texas Association of Realtors' Seller's Disclosure Notice: ***YOU ARE ENCOURAGED TO HAVE INSPECTOR OF YOUR CHOICE INSPECT PROPERTY.*** Choose the inspector yourself, have the home inspected, and go over the inspection report with the inspector. Just do it. Follow *Step 4* and you will be able to close the deal with the confidence that you are purchasing the kind of home you intended to purchase.

———

CHAPTER VI

Step 5: Don't Rely On The Seller's Disclosure Notice Or The MLS Report—These Documents Do Not Protect You

The Seller's Disclosure Notice

In previous chapters, I have mentioned the Seller's Disclosure Notice. Texas law requires the seller of a residential property to complete what is called a Seller's Disclosure Notice. The theory behind the disclosure notice is that the sellers have lived in the house and they know more about the home than anyone else. The Texas legislature decided that sellers should disclose on a form what they know about the home's history and condition. The notice is usually four pages of relatively small print. The form contains sections, with each section addressing certain elements of the particular home covered by the notice. There's a section that simply lists the items that will be conveyed with the property. There's one for

listing malfunctions in certain items like plumbing, heating, and electrical systems. There's another for stating whether the seller is aware of any conditions like asbestos, radon gas, soil movement, settling, and a host of other conditions. There's a section that asks if the seller is aware that any of the listed items is in need of repair, and so on. The seller is asked to check a box whether he or she is aware of any defects in the system. The box is marked yes or no. And then the seller goes down the list and checks off each item.

The seller should and probably will provide a copy of the disclosure notice to the potential home buyer before the Earnest Money Contract is signed. The buyer's real estate agent will usually get the disclosure notice from the seller's agent, or the notice will be provided at the home the first time the potential buyer looks at the property. The buyer then goes over the form to get an idea of the condition of the home. The disclosure notice may alert the buyer to major problems with the home. Although the list of things checked off is not extraordinarily long, most buyers and their agents do not go over the list in detail. Usually what happens is that the buyer will go over the list to see if the seller had checked any "yes" boxes or placed a Y next to an item. Since this means there is some sort of problem, the buyer will want to know about the problem.

Sellers obviously read the seller's disclosure notice from their perspective. What does *defect* mean? *Defect* may have different meanings for

different people. Some sellers, for example, can live with a loud noise every time the air conditioner turns on, and would not consider that a defect. Most buyers, on the other hand, would not want the loud noise of an air conditioning unit to sound every time it turns on. The cost of the repair may be minimal or it may be major. No one will know the cost until a repair person comes out to analyze the problem. But after the deal is closed, it is too late for the buyer to then ask the question. Further, if you find out about the problem after your unrestricted right to terminate has expired, it may be too late to insist that the problem be repaired before the sale is closed.

Whenever there is any doubt whatsoever about whether the problem is a defect, the seller should err on the side of calling the problem a defect. Usually the problem can be worked out to where everyone is happy and the deal closes. The guiding light for sellers here is: Disclose, Disclose, Disclose, Disclose. Full disclosure is the best protection available to a seller against complaints or a suit by a dissatisfied buyer.

The most important bit of information to be aware of regarding the Seller's Disclosure Notice is that the notice is good only for **THE DAY ON WHICH IT WAS SIGNED!** This is what the print says at the top of the page. If, down the road, you as the buyer attempt to claim that the seller somehow had misled you about claiming there was no defect in the air conditioner, you will most likely have

to prove that on the day the seller signed the notice, the air conditioner was defective. Not the day before and not the day after. This is a very difficult burden, as you may well imagine. Say the house has been on the market for two months. Usually, the disclosure notice is completed and signed by the seller before the home is placed in the multiple listing used by most real estate agents. Then consider that you purchase the home in March and don't use the air conditioner until May. Also consider all the time that will lapse between the time you make a demand that the seller repair the item, the seller refuses your demand, you hire an attorney, the attorney files suit, and he or she begins investigating the facts to help win your case. Obviously, you cannot count on the person who sold the home to state that yes, the air conditioner was defective on the day that he or she completed the form, and a mistake was made. The most realistic scenario is that the seller will state under oath that he or she had never heard any kind of a noise that was loud or obnoxious enough to be considered a defect, at the time the notice was completed.

The point of all this is that you as the buyer must realize that the Seller's Disclosure Notice is good only for the day of the signing.

Review the disclosure notice with your spouse or friend. Don't hurry when reviewing the notice. Regardless of what is checked, underline all items that are important to you. Take into consideration the age of the house, the amount you're paying for the house, your finances, and determine whether you want to incur the expense of repairing any defective items or systems in the home. If you think you can handle the expense of a new water heater or rewiring job, for example, then don't be concerned about that. If you feel you don't wish to handle such expenses, then highlight that item, and so on.

There is a section in the Texas Realtors Association* disclosure notice that requires the seller to disclose previous inspections of the property that have been performed by licensed professionals such as inspectors, engineers, electricians, plumbers, and the like. The seller is also required to provide copies of any reports made by these inspectors. It is essential that you receive copies of these reports. If the seller discloses a prior inspection, make absolutely certain you get a copy of the report right away. This report is a vital part of your inspection. You must give a copy of the report to your inspector before he inspects the property. The importance of such reports to your due diligence cannot be stressed enough. This is another item that is not negotiable. You must have these reports. If a seller refuses to provide copies of these reports, you must walk away from the deal. If you can't walk away, chances are, you're already in a bad deal.

When you have thoroughly gone through the disclosure notice and highlighted everything that is important to you, call your real estate agent and have him or her schedule the face-to-face meeting with the seller, which I discussed somewhat in Chapter II. In addition to your other concerns, your concerns highlighted in the disclosure notice should be discussed at that meeting. Ask questions about all of the things you're concerned about. Remember, the seller wants to sell the home. You are probably making the one of the largest purchases you will make over your lifetime, and it's your money being spent.

This should not be a confrontational meeting where you are questioning the credibility of the seller. The seller's credibility is of no concern to you as a buyer. You're not relying on trust. You're merely taking precaution based on the fact that that you're aware that the disclosure notice is good only on the day that it was signed. You're also aware that the sellers have made no representations to your agent or to the seller's agent about the condition of the home, other than what was represented in the Seller's Disclosure Notice. These are the reasons the opportunity to talk to the seller is necessary and must be taken advantage of. You as a buyer will want to know a little more about your specific concerns and those certain items in the disclosure notice that you have underlined.

If a seller is reluctant to sit down with you and discuss these items, this is a red flag to be aware of right away. If your real estate agent says you cannot do that or that he or she will not or cannot schedule the meeting, that is also a red flag which you must take notice of immediately. You as the buyer are entitled to know as much about the property you're purchasing as you want to know. Any attempts to hinder your access to information that should be readily available through a discussion with the sellers should cause you great concern. You should begin looking for another property, you should engage another real estate agent, or both. You as the buyer simply cannot under any circumstances purchase a home without knowing all the information you can about the portions of the home that are important to you. The failure to obtain the information to which you are entitled and which you have an opportunity to obtain is at your own risk.

Recall that at the top of the Seller's Disclosure Notice in all capital letters are the words NOT A WARRANTY OF ANY KIND. This means that on the form, the seller is stating only what he or she is aware of at the time the form is completed. The seller is not stating on the form that any appliance or system in the home will work properly for even one more day. If, on the form, the seller states that the air conditioner is working, all that means is that on the day the seller filled out the disclosure notice, the air conditioner was, in fact, working. The same goes for every representation made in the seller's disclosure notice. The seller is not making any representations about the future performance of anything. You must understand this. To determine the future performance of any appliances or systems in the home, you must conduct your own inspection or hire your own inspector to perform the inspection.

If you would be terribly disturbed to find that a person had died in the home, you must ask the sellers. Don't wait to hear it from neighbors after you move in.

THE MLS REPORT

The Multiple Listing Service (MLS) report contains information about the home that is provided to the seller's broker by the seller. The purpose of the MLS report is to assist real estate agents in locating homes for their clients. The buyer's agent uses the MLS report to match up homes in an area the agent feels would meet the desired criteria that the agent has been given by the buyer. If the buyer desires a 2,500-square-foot two-bedroom home with a pool, located in a gated community on the outskirts of town, within thirty minutes' drive from downtown, in the $350,000 price range, the agent will first go to the MLS to search for properties that meet or come close to those criteria. MLS reports are not under any circumstances to be relied on by the buyer for representations about the quality or condition of the home, or the square footage of the home itself, or the lot. At the bottom of the MLS report, you'll find language similar to the following:

> All measurements, taxes, age, financial, and school data are approximate and provided by other sources. Buyer should independently verify same before relying thereon.

The only reason for a potential home buyer to look at an MLS report is to get a general idea of whether you would be interested in looking at the property. The MLS report is designed to save time hunting for the right property. That is all it is to be used for — nothing else. These reports always contain words like "new," "great," "updated," "lovely," "perfect," "nice," "relaxing," "private," "secluded," "quiet," and a host of similar words. The only reason brokers use words like these is to get potential buyers to look at the property. What you must understand here is that what is a "lovely" view to the seller's broker may not be a "lovely" view to you. What is an "updated" kitchen to the seller's broker may not be an "updated" kitchen to you. What seems like a "perfect" back yard for entertaining to the seller's broker may not seem like a "perfect" back yard for entertaining to you.

If you're in the market for a home with a "perfect" back yard for entertaining, then look for a home that has a "perfect" back yard for entertaining as you see it. If a "perfect" back yard for entertaining to you is one that is secluded with tall trees, a natural pond with fish, paved walkways, an outdoor kitchen, and a wood-burning oven, then look for a home that has a back yard that meets those criteria. If you find a home that fits, then go and sit in the back yard, relax, and spend time looking around. Imagine yourself hosting a dinner party in that back yard. Get a feel for what it would be like having friends over for an informal barbeque. If you look up and see tall trees blowing in the wind, look around and see woods and thicket and cannot see your neighbor's home, but you can see the fish swimming in the natural pond when you get up from your chair to walk on the paved walkway to the pond, and see the wood stacked by the wood-burning oven that is part of the outdoor kitchen, then you yourself establish that this home has the "perfect" back yard for entertaining. You are not relying on someone else to establish that for you.

If you buy the home, it will be yours. It will belong to you. You will have to maintain it. You and your family are the ones who will have to live in it. You will have to eat and sleep and entertain in it. Since you are the one who will be doing all of these things — not the seller's broker — make certain that it is the "perfect" home for you based on your criteria and your requirements. This is the only place in your home purchase where you can rely on trust — trust in yourself. Trust yourself here and you can't go wrong.

TRUST YOURSELF

Don't rely or depend on the Seller's Disclosure Notice for assurance about the condition or quality of the home, or any system in it, or any appliance. Don't rely on the MLS Report for anything more than to give you the location of the home, asking price, and a general idea of the specifics. Under *Step 5*, trust yourself to purchase the perfect home for you. Do this and you will close with the confidence that you'll be happy with your purchase.

————————

CHAPTER VII

STEP 6: ALWAYS RESEARCH THE NEIGHBORHOOD YOURSELF

Almost all home buyers will hear statements from the seller, the broker, or the agent that the neighborhood is "nice," the schools are "great," we've never had "any problems," the church is around the corner, and so forth. The main thing to consider in listening to these statements is that none of them mean anything to you as the buyer. A nice neighborhood to you may be a neighborhood where there are not a lot of children. A nice neighborhood to someone else may mean that it has a lot of trees. Great schools to one person may mean that they have good football teams every year. To another person, great schools may mean that the majority of students graduate. To a third, great schools may mean 80 percent of graduating seniors go on to college. Not having had "any problems" to one person may mean there's no drag racing on the street late at night. To another, not having had "any problems" may mean that there haven't been any thefts of lawnmowers from garages in the area. You can see what I am aiming at here. You must research the neighborhood yourself.

If you're planning on having your children walk to school, then make the effort to walk from the home to the school and back yourself. Make the walk even if it is only a block or two. You'll be surprised at what you see when you're walking, as opposed to being in a car. You may walk by an alley that you did not even see when you drove by. The alley may contain trash and other unsightly items, which you do not wish your child to have to walk past.

"There are no registered sex offenders within a ten-mile radius of the home" is a statement that has meaning. This is a statement you can check. Some Seller's Disclosure statements will contain language stating that the buyer should check this him- or herself. Checking for registered sex offenders is simple. Just get on the Internet and go to the site in your state. If you go to my Web site, I have provided links to the sites in all fifty states for locating registered sex offenders.

You may not like the sound of airplanes landing and taking off. When you visit the home, the wind may be blowing in a direction that changes the landing and take-off pattern so that you did not hear any planes while you were there. But the next day (at the same time you visited the day before), a plane takes off every two minutes — and at the home you're considering purchasing, the jet engine noise makes the windows rattle. Due to the direction of the wind on your earlier visit, you were not aware of the noise. If airplane noise concerns you because the house you're considering buying is near an airport, then you must check with the seller, the neighbors, and the airport for the flight patterns. Once you close the deal and are awakened unexpectedly the first morning in your newly purchased home, it will be too late to complain about airplane noise.

The same goes for trains, freeways, buses, and heavy trucks. If you do not want to listen to this kind of noise, then make certain you spend enough time at the property and ask sufficient questions of the sellers and their neighbors about these kinds of noises so you have a good idea of what you can expect. If, after you close the deal and have moved into your newly purchased home, you discover the 2 AM train horn wakes you up when it sounds every night as it passes the crossing a quarter mile away, it is too late to complain.

You may have to commute to work from the home you're in the process of buying. Don't rely on your agent's statement that the traffic is not bad from the home to your workplace. If traffic is a concern to you and you don't like driving in stop-and-go traffic every day, then check the traffic yourself. Go to the property at the time you plan to travel to work, and make the trip during that time. Do this on two or three different work days so you can see for yourself what the traffic is like. Only then will you know what it is really like. The effort of spending a few days to get this information will pale in comparison to the effort you may have to spend trying to resell the home because you cannot put up with the stop-and-go traffic every day you commute to work — not to mention your daily discomfort with the drive.

Anything that is important to you about the location of the home, you must check yourself. Finding out information about things of this importance must not be delegated. It's your responsibility to make certain that all aspects of the home's location fit your requirements. Take the time to check the neighborhood yourself. If you find that you can blame someone else for your dislike of the location, then you have not performed your responsibility. Once you have reached the point when you can say to yourself, "If I am not satisfied with this location, then I have only myself to blame," you can close the deal knowing you met your responsibilities regarding the home's location. By following *Step 6*, you will place yourself in a position to close the deal with the confidence that you have selected the right location for you and your family.

———————

CHAPTER VIII:

STEP 7: THE CONDITION OF THE HOME MUST MEET THE TERMS OF THE EARNEST MONEY CONTRACT. IF IT DOESN'T, DO NOT CLOSE.

Shortly before you go to closing, you'll be asked to perform a walk-through of the home for a final inspection. Do not take this inspection lightly. Open and close the doors, turn the lights off and on, flush the commodes, turn on the hot and cold water, open and close the windows, check the garbage disposal, ovens, stove tops, gas operated fireplaces, check the water heater, open the closets, open the cabinets, check the smoke detectors, check the security alarms, open and close the garage doors, look under the sink in the bathrooms and in the kitchen, check the operation of the filter systems in the pool, hot tub, and ponds, and make certain all cleaning and repairs that you negotiated for and that are written in the Earnest Money Contract or in any addendum attached to the contract have, in fact, been completed.

As I stated to you earlier, upon completing this inspection, you'll be asked to sign the Texas Association of Realtors' Buyer's "Walk Thru" and Acceptance form. Pay attention to and understand this document. This is a very important document, as are all of the others discussed in this book. In virtually all purchases of a home, the buyer will sign a document like this. When you as the buyer sign this document, you're essentially representing to anyone who reads the document that you have inspected the property and that you found it to be in the condition you wanted it to be, in order for you to close the deal. You also represent when you sign this form that you fully understand that it is your (the buyer's) responsibility to have the inspection of the home completed. And since you have acknowledged in writing your responsibility to inspect the property, you'd better have the appropriate inspection done.

By signing the Buyer's "Walk Thru" and Acceptance form, you aren't representing that you trusted the sellers, or that you trusted the brokers, or that you trusted the agents. You're representing that you understand that you are the one responsible for inspecting this home, that you know you are the one responsible for inspecting, that you have not relied on anyone else to inspect the home for you, and that having signed this document and the Earnest Money Contract, you are accepting the property "AS IS."

Having represented this in writing for all to see, you'd better have accomplished what you have represented, not just so your own integrity remains intact, but so you make certain you are purchasing what you had contracted to purchase. Spending a few hours or days backing up the documents you are signing will — in the long run, should a problem with the home arise — save you tens of thousands of dollars, countless hours of arguments and frustration, and possibly months or years of litigation.

When you get to closing, ask yourself: "Have I relied on hope to get through the details, or did I make an informed decision? Does the water heater work? Is the electrical system up to snuff? Are there any pipes leaking underground? Does the heating and air-conditioning unit make a loud noise every time it goes on? Does the roof leak? Are the commodes in good working order? What about termites and rats? Have I asked the sellers if they had an exterminator? If so, who? Was I able to talk to the exterminator? What about the windows? Do they keep out the rain and other weather elements? Is the heating unit the correct size for the house? Does the foundation warranty transfer to me as the buyer? Did I get a chance to talk to the sellers? Did I get all of the previous inspection reports? Did I give them to my inspector before he inspected the property? Did I go over the inspection report with my inspector? Did I select the inspector after checking his or her credentials and reputation? Did I check the neighborhood myself? Have I performed a thorough walk-through inspection right before closing? Did I have enough time for the inspection or was I rushed? Were all of my questions answered? Was I given access to all areas of the home?"

Did you leave any of these matters up to your agent? Did you trust the agent to give you accurate information? Are you hoping you will not find any problems after you close? Did you not ask the agent any questions because you didn't wish to upset the agent? If you don't raise these questions or others like them, then you're relying on hope and trust: "She seems honest." "He seems like a nice person." "His son is in the Boy Scouts with my son." "What reason do I have to be concerned?" If we cannot honestly say to ourselves that we are making an informed decision to purchase the home, we must not close the sale. The risk we take is too great. Better to lose the $100 option fee for terminating the contract than to pay $10,000 to repair a water-damaged floor infested with mold.

You can see by now, I'm sure, that trust and hope have no place in the purchase of your home. The "in its present condition" clause in the TREC form contract prohibits any purchaser from going forward on the basis of trust and hope. America wasn't built on trust and hope. Don't purchase your piece of

America on the basis of trust and hope. Unscrupulous sellers, agents, and brokers will try to make you feel uncomfortable when you take actions necessary to back up the representations you are making when you sign the documents required to purchase your home. Such people will try to pressure you to hurry. This kind of pressure will be most evident if you want to delay the closing because the condition of the home is not what you had contracted for. Should you feel the least bit pressured, you must immediately recognize a red flag. A good agent or broker will stand behind you, even if it means the closing must be delayed or the contract must be terminated and the hunt for a home begun once again. In the big picture, these kinds of things are minor and are part of purchasing a home. The reputable agent and broker are building their reputations and they want repeat business. They want you to refer other potential home buyers to them. Consequently, they'll bend over backwards to ensure that all of the representations you make on the documents signed in the transaction are backed up with your diligent search for information about the history and condition of the home and its appliances and systems.

Before you close, take time in the final walk-through inspection to verify the condition of the home you are about to purchase. Make certain that the home is in the condition you intended it to be in at the time of purchase. If you bargained for the carpets to be cleaned, make certain they have been cleaned.

If you bargained for the roof to be repaired, make certain the roof has been repaired. If you bargained for the drainage to be adjusted, make certain that has been done. Make certain that everything you had bargained for has been completed before you close. If the condition of the property does not meet terms you had bargained for in your Earnest Money Contract, DO NOT CLOSE — PERIOD! If you do, you will have wasted your efforts to close the deal with confidence, which you had carefully expended in the previous six steps.

Once you sign the closing papers at the title company or other place of closing, you have effectively closed the "AS IS" purchase of your home. At this juncture, all leverage you may have had to get the seller to comply with the Earnest Money Contract is lost. I can tell you from experience with numerous persons who have called my firm seeking assistance, that it is like pulling teeth to get a seller to do anything with the home after closing. Once the deal closes, all sellers feel like they have nothing more to do with the property. Don't fight this reality. Keep the seller in the game until you have received everything you bargained to receive. Only then should you close. Only then can you close with confidence.

———————

CHAPTER IX:

PROTECTION AGAINST A BAD DEAL
FOLLOW THE 7 EASY STEPS

It is entirely possible for someone to follow the *7 Easy Steps* in this book and still purchase a home with a major problem. What then? Fortunately for those who suffer such a disaster, there is an avenue for relief, but if AND ONLY IF the agent, the broker, or the seller committed fraud that can be proven with evidence that is credible. An example of this kind of circumstance is where the agent, broker, or seller had actual knowledge of a material defect in the home, but then intentionally failed to disclose the problem to the buyer for the purpose of inducing the buyer to purchase the home. The same would apply if any one of these individuals intentionally hid the problem from discovery, to induce the buyer to close the transaction.

While fraud committed by agents, brokers, or sellers is not common, such untoward conduct does occur. Most of the time when a buyer is defrauded, the hidden or undisclosed defect that the perpetrator knew about is substantial. Homes with foundation problems make up a sizeable portion of homes involving fraud. Sticking doors and cracking in the interior walls and ceilings usually indicate foundation defects. As the foundation moves, cracks appear and stay, or they open and close. A seller who wants to hide these cracks can easily have the cracks repaired and the rooms in which the cracks are repaired repainted. The cracks that open and close may not be open during the day the seller completes the seller's disclosure notice. The cracks may not be visible when you inspect the home. The seller may also indicate on the notice that the home never had any foundation problems. Since the walls are newly painted and there is no other evidence of foundation problems, you as the buyer, your inspector, and all who walk through the home will have no reason to determine that the home had suffered from past foundation problems. Additionally, in your informal meeting with the seller, you brought up the question but the seller denied there were any foundation problems.

But within weeks of moving into the home, cracks begin appearing in the walls and you realize there is a problem. You then call your real estate agent and he or she says there is nothing that can be done. You call the broker and he or she says there is nothing he or she can do. You call the seller and the seller refuses to return your calls. Then you find out from your new neighbor that the home you purchased had foundation problems for years. You learn that the sellers had to repair the entire kitchen tile on the floor because it cracked, and that is why the kitchen has new all-weather carpeting instead of tile on the floor. You learn that the seller had foundation repair companies at the home to give repair bids. You learn that the owner had a soaker hose outside of the foundation the previous summer.

In this scenario, buyers unaware of their duties and responsibilities under the contracts they signed will feel cheated by the sellers, by the real estate agent, and by the inspector. The system which gave the buyers a feeling of confidence and protection is about to turn against them. The buyers feel that they hired a real estate agent to protect their interests, an inspector to protect their interests, an appraiser to protect their interests, and relied on real estate forms approved by the Texas Real Estate Commission or the Texas Association of Realtors˙ to protect their interests. With all of this protection, how could it possibly happen that they had purchased a home with foundation problems, which will cost thousands of dollars to repair? Again, the reason will be that the buyer probably relied on trust for protection.

When a problem is discovered after moving in, the buyer will usually call the real estate agent. The agent is really of no help, because the deal is closed. The agent has his or her commission. There is nothing left for the agent to do. The common response from the real estate agent is: "I really can't help you on this matter. It appears that the seller has misled us. You may want to call an attorney to see what recourse you may have against the seller." But you don't want to pursue a lawsuit. That is the last thing you want.

When there is a problem discovered after the closing and the buyers are rebuffed at every turn while trying to get help, the buyers have nowhere else to go but to an attorney. The attorney then sets up an appointment and asks the buyers to bring in all of their paperwork involved in the purchase. The buyers bring in the closing documents that they signed at the title company, including the Earnest Money Contract, the Seller's Disclosure Notice, the Inspection Report, the Buyers' "Walk Thru" and Acceptance form, and the agreement between the buyer and the real estate agent. After reviewing all of the paperwork, the attorney will usually tell the unhappy buyers there is nothing that can be done, because all of the paperwork that the buyers had signed — thinking it would protect them against any problems with the new home — in actuality, protected the agent, broker, and seller from liability for damages suffered by the buyers. The end result is that the paperwork protected everyone but the buyers. After reviewing the paperwork, the attorney usually ends up telling the buyers that they are out of luck and are going to have to suffer the loss.

Sometimes, however, the attorney feels that the protections afforded everyone except the buyer are technically defective or that the protections have been waived by some conduct of the individuals — for example, fraud. Rarely, if ever, is the home buyer satisfied once litigation commences. Litigation is long and cumbersome. Everyone involved on the defense side completely digs in their heels and prominently displays the small print and the shields against liability in all of the documents, along with the new buyer's signatures.

In the end, what was supposed to have been a dream home, the American dream, has turned into a never-ending nightmare. I have seen such bad purchases result in fights, failed marriages, bankruptcies, and severe psychological distress resulting in hospitalization. I have seen a home buyer trapped by the documents he signed left with a $250,000 mortgage on a home worth only $120,000 because of undisclosed foundation problems. And it doesn't have to be a foundation problem. It could be a roof problem, a problem with the electrical system, a plumbing problem, or any other such problem. I have seen a family purchase a home for $1.2 million, only to be saddled with a $350,000 repair bill because the pillars supporting a large living room overlooking a scenic ravine were engineered improperly. Do not let this happen to you. Follow the *7 Easy Steps* and this won't happen to you.

You performed your due diligence, just as required in the pages of this book. You asked all of the right questions of the broker, agent, and sellers. You hired your own inspector. You discussed the inspection report with the inspector. You thoroughly inspected the home during the option and then again when you performed the final walk-through inspection — and there were no indications of foundation problems. If you can say to yourself with confidence, "I have done everything I reasonably could do to search for and discover defects in the purchased residence," then your legal claims will stand on a foundation of considerable strength.

You don't wish to pursue a lawsuit — the whole purpose behind this book is to protect you from undergoing a lawsuit. But sometimes a lawsuit cannot be avoided. If you unfortunately happen to have been defrauded, following the *7 Easy Steps* in this book will place you on the right side of any suit over the matter, and no language in any of the documents you signed can be used in the perpetrator's defense. The TREC documents do not protect sellers, agents, or brokers against fraud. In fact, the contrary is true. If we as buyers understand our duties and obligations, as set out in the TREC documents used in a residential real estate transaction, and we fulfill those duties and obligations, that conduct will not only protect us against any defenses the perpetrator attempts to raise against a fraud claim, the actions we have taken will actually produce all of the evidence necessary to prove our claims of fraud against the perpetrator, whether it be the agent, the broker, or the seller.

By following the *7 Easy Steps* in this book, if an unbargained-for defect surfaces after closing, you will have made your case for fraud. We can protect against fraud but we can't prevent it. While a lawsuit is not what anyone wants when they purchase a home, you can take comfort knowing you have the evidence to prove your case and that you are not trapped by language in the documents that you had signed to make the purchase. If you must be in a lawsuit, then this is the position you want to be in.

———————

CHAPTER X:

ALWAYS CLOSE WITH CONFIDENCE

When we delve into a real estate transaction armed with the knowledge of what the contract means and how it is interpreted by the courts, we as buyers negotiate from a solid bargaining position. We as buyers can then negotiate on the basis of objective reality — not on the basis of hope or trust. This is because we absolutely know that if we don't properly inspect the property, if we don't ask questions about items that concern us — such as the age of the roof — we most likely will have no recourse against a seller, an agent, or a broker who is less than truthful. Remember that the Earnest Money Contract we will sign to begin the purchase process is an "AS IS" contract. Remember also that the documents we sign throughout the purchase process and at closing solidly place the burden on us to discover defects in the home. These documents effectively prevent us from trusting the agent, seller, or broker to bring defects to light, and also prevent us from hoping that all defects will surface. This knowledge forces us to act accordingly. Our actions of research and due diligence will give us the confidence we must have in order to make prudent decisions regarding the condition and quality of the home, its systems, and appliances that we are about to purchase.

Don't be shy about asking the seller to provide you the names of any repair persons who worked on the home in the previous five years. Also ask the seller if you may have permission to talk to these repair persons. Then call the repair person and ask questions about the repairs: "What was the reason for the repairs?" "Was there a permit that the repair person had to pull from the city or county in order to make the repairs?" "Was the permit actually pulled?" "Were the repairs performed properly?" "How long are the repairs expected to last?" These and similar questions must be asked about situations where the condition or quality of the item gives you cause for concern. Before the transaction moves forward, you must have the answers.

You should also not hesitate to ask to speak to the sellers and ask any questions you have about the condition or quality of the home. This approach is a must. No one in the transaction will know more about the quality and condition of the home than will the sellers. Honest sellers will not be put off by such questions. They will gladly give you the information. They know that everything you discover will be consistent what they have been telling you about the house. Their representations will be in line with what was disclosed in the Seller's Disclosure Notice. Everything will fit nicely together, like a puzzle. The previous history of the home will come to light. What you learn will correspond with what you have been told and will lead to you making an informed decision when it comes time to close the deal.

Making an informed decision, that is, a decision based on objective reality, is the single most important factor in purchasing a home that you will be happy with. When you make a decision based solely on trusting others, you're asking for trouble. A major and obvious red flag is for an agent, broker, or seller to make you feel uncomfortable on the grounds that you do not trust him or her. The fact that you were made to feel uncomfortable is in and of itself a reason to get to the bottom of why you feel uncomfortable. Honest agents, brokers, and sellers will welcome your questions and will answer them openly and directly. There is nothing for them to hide. They will not expect you to simply trust them. In fact, the best and most respectable agents and brokers will encourage you to ask questions and to obtain as much information as you can about the condition and quality of the home. You shouldn't feel uncomfortable about asking questions. Discussions with your spouse, for example, may sound something like this: "Dr. and

Mrs. Jones seem like honest people. They don't look like the kind of people who would hide anything from us. They don't seem like they would try to cheat us. After all, their kids go to the same school as our kids." Or, "I'm in the PTA with her sister, and her sister is really a nice person" or "They go to the same church as my parents" or "We both graduated from the same high school." If any one of these or similar facts leads you to not ask questions for fear of upsetting the person you're asking, it will almost always lead to problems, heartache, disappointment, and even loss of friendships down the road. It's likely that problems will arise if you fail to ask questions for fear of upsetting or hurting the agent's, broker's, or seller's feelings. Ironically, your questions might lead to an undiscovered problem that could be easily resolved prior to purchase.

Say the dishwasher breaks down two weeks after you close and move into your new home. On top of all of the other fees and expenses you had to pay for closing the deal, you now are facing the cost of a new dishwasher. You may review the Seller's Disclosure Notice and see a check mark in the box that nothing was wrong with the dishwasher. Maybe at the time the box was checked, there was nothing wrong with the dishwasher — and between then and the time you closed, the seller did not have a problem with it. You never asked how old the dishwasher was or whether it had ever broken down while the sellers lived in the house. The answer to your question, as long as it was honest, might have brought to the surface a problem that came up after the disclosure notice was completed. If the sellers had told you the dishwasher was twenty-five years old or that it had to be repaired four months ago, you may have negotiated down the price by $500. Or you may not have. You may have still closed the transaction knowing the age of the dishwasher or knowing it had been repaired recently. The point is that you will have closed the deal with confidence.

When you close with confidence, you don't look to place blame on anyone for having purchased a defective home. You don't have to place blame on anyone because you know all about the quality and condition of the home before you sign the closing documents. When you close with confidence, you will have no reason to place blame. When you close with confidence, and you're defrauded, you will still not have to place blame — the law places the blame for you. When you close a home purchase with confidence, you close fully informed.

Decisions in a home purchase based on hope and trust are weak and troublesome decisions. Hope, like trust, has no place in the purchase of a home. You are not hoping to purchase a home. You actually *are* going to purchase the home. You have worked hard. You have saved. You have reached the stage in your life where you can afford to purchase your dream home. The home is an object that you can see, feel, and touch. You can walk around it. You can look at each of the rooms. You can see the attic. You can watch the sun gleam off the windows. You don't *hope* to see these things. They're there. They are visible the first time you see the home.

Buyers who experience problems down the road — after closing when nothing can be done — often trade their diligence to inspect, for hope and trust during the period of looking for the right home. The agent is very nice. The agent is saying a lot of nice things: "This is thte right home for you. I know you are going to love this home. That room will be a perfect play room for your daughter. The neighborhood has a lot of kids in it, and the elementary school is right down the street." When you sit down and consider these statements, they don't give you any information about the history or condition of the home. All of these statements seem to make sense to you. So you and your husband go home and talk about how close the school will be for Mindy when she turns five. You talk about how the room is perfect for Mindy. How the yard is fenced and how you will be able to put up a swing set. And you are excited about moving in. The agent has shown you several houses. You want to tell all of your friends about your new home. You are about to purchase a piece of America, on top of which sits your special home.

Be a satisfied buyer. Follow the *7 Easy Steps*. Buy your home fully informed. Close the deal with confidence. Gain valuable appreciation on your investment. Live the American Dream.

CARL PIPOLY - ATTORNEY

After graduating Magna Cum Laude from the University of Denver, Carl Pipoly earned his law degree from the University of Denver College of Law in 1980. He then went to work for Conoco Oil Company, where he was responsible for negotiating and drafting joint venture agreements with French, German, and Japanese companies, covering multimillion-dollar exploration and minerals production facilities in the United States, Canada, South America, and Africa.

Pipoly founded Pipoly Law Offices in 1989 after selling Conquista Project Corporation, a company he founded in 1985. In his law practice he has represented thousands of homebuyers in many different kinds of claims. He has tried over 100 cases to verdict before a jury.

He is a member of the Texas and Colorado bars; the United States District Courts for the Northern, Eastern and Western Districts of Texas and the Colorado District; and the United States Court of Appeals for the Fifth and Seventh Circuits. A member of the

Texas Trial Lawyers Association and the San Antonio Trial Lawyers Association, he is recognized as an Advocate with the National College of Advocacy.

An accomplished athlete, Pipoly successfully swam the English Channel in 1980 and was a champion bicycle racer. He is married and has four children.

www.ingramcontent.com/pod-product-compliance
Lightning Source LLC
Chambersburg PA
CBHW022114170526
45157CB00004B/1628